# Contents

Global warming 4

Is the climate changing? 6

A greenhouse world 12

Weather watch 20

Climatic consequences 24

Biological changes 32

Combating the changes 38

Living with global warming 52

Conclusion 56

Timeline 58

Glossary 60

Sources of information 63

Index 64

Any words appearing in the text in bold, **like this**, are explained in the Glossary.

# Global warming

The first year of the new millennium witnessed several unusual **weather** events. The worst floods in hundreds of years struck Madagascar, Mozambique and southern Africa. Heavy rains also occurred in other places, too. Western Australia experienced record rainfall. The extra-heavy **monsoon** in South and South-East Asia brought floods in which more than 650 people died, and 10 million people were affected in India alone. Torrential rains and deadly mudslides wreaked havoc in Central and South America in May and June. Later in the year it was no better. There was severe flooding in the Alps, the United Kingdom and France. In contrast, a scorching heatwave gripped much of southern Europe during June and July of that year, breaking many records and claiming numerous lives as temperatures soared to 43°C in Greece, Italy, Romania and Turkey.

During 2000 there was extensive flooding in much of Mozambique, including Xai-Xai province shown here, as rivers and streams burst their banks.

The 20th century ended with an average global temperature that was 0.6 degrees Celsius higher than the start of the century. This increase in average global temperature was the largest of any century over the last 1000 years. The year 2000 was the sixth warmest year of a 140-year period dating back to 1860. The warmer years were 1998, 1997, 1995, 1990 and 1999.

Many people believe that the changes in the weather are due to **global warming**. Global warming is the term used to describe the increase in the average global temperature. The Earth is warming up because certain gases in the atmosphere are on the increase, including carbon dioxide and methane. Global warming is an issue that affects everybody in the world and it has to be tackled by all countries.

In this book you can learn about the **greenhouse effect**, the role of the **greenhouse gases** and why these gases are on the increase. You can find out how the world **climate** could change as global temperatures increase and what effects these changes may have on plant and animal life, crops and people. In the latter part of the book you can read about how individuals and governments could reduce greenhouse gas emissions and start to combat these changes.

The beaches of the Mediterranean are popular with tourists, but in recent years temperatures during the summer have risen above 40°C, threatening the health of visitors.

# Is the climate changing?

Climate change is not new. During the last Ice Age that ended about 10,000 years ago, average global temperatures were five or so degrees Celsius below those of today. The end of the Ice Age was marked by a period of relatively rapid warming, bringing the world's average temperature to a level similar to that of today, that is 15°C. For the last 10,000 years, average global temperatures have not varied by much more than a degree either side of 15°C.

Two thousand years ago, Greenland was much warmer than today and it was covered by lush vegetation, giving the area its name. Then the climate became cooler, the vegetation was lost and the ice sheet extended over the land. Between 1430 and 1850, northern Europe experienced a 'Little Ice Age'. During this time, the climate was much colder and crops failed. There were widespread food shortages and starvation.

Britain experienced some of its coldest winters during the 1810s and 1820s. The River Thames froze regularly and Frost Fairs were held on its icy surface. The year 1816 was described as the year without summer, with frosts in June and disastrous crop failures.

## Rising temperatures

Although there have been temperature fluctuations in the past, a definite upward trend is emerging. Continuous records dating back 140 years show that the 1990s was the warmest decade on record. The warmest years on record are, in descending order, 1998, 1997, 1995, 1990, 1999 and 2000.

This rise in global temperatures has led scientists to believe that something is causing the climate to change. The most likely cause is an increase in the quantities of greenhouse gases in the atmosphere. These gases trap heat in the atmosphere, and as they increase in concentration they cause the global temperatures to increase. This increase is called global warming.

Modern power stations can burn coal, gas or oil to generate electricity. A network of pylons and cables carry the electricity to the consumer.

Since the beginning of the **Industrial Revolution**, about 250 years ago, increasing quantities of **fossil fuels** have been burnt. When these fuels burn they release carbon dioxide, a greenhouse gas. The rise in the use of fossil fuels has been accompanied by an overall increase in global temperatures.

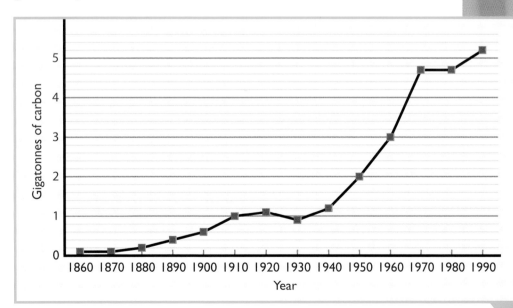

This graph shows the global increase in fossil fuel use from 1860 to 1990. The trend is still rising.

## Looking for evidence

Just over ten years ago, the idea of global warming was mostly theoretical – the evidence for it was still unclear. Many governments decided not to take any action until there was real evidence. In 2001 the Intergovernmental Panel on Climate Change (**IPCC**), which had been set up by the United Nations, published its latest report. This stated that the trend towards a warmer world had begun. Its scientists had analysed data going back hundreds of years on everything from air and water temperatures to the distribution of plants and animals. They found that this warming had an impact on more than 400 different processes, both physical and biological, on all continents. The panel concluded that the significant increase in the temperature of the world was linked to human activity.

The ice sheet of the Arctic is breaking up earlier than normal in spring every year. This affects the shelters used by polar bears and hampers their hunting activities.

Today there is a wealth of evidence for global warming:
- measured increases in average temperatures
- changing rainfall patterns
- rising sea levels
- glaciers thinning and retreating
- coral reefs dying as the oceans become warmer
- more frequent droughts in Africa and Asia
- permafrost (the permanent frozen ground) melting in the Arctic
- lakes and rivers that freeze in winter thawing earlier each year
- plants and animals shifting their ranges towards the poles and to higher altitudes
- disrupted migration patterns for animals, such as whales and polar bears.

These observations are undeniably pointing to a changing climate. One drought or freak weather event may not be caused by global warming, but the sheer number of events suggests that it is real – it is happening.

## The Kyoto Protocol

In recent years, the word 'Kyoto' has been linked with global warming and international climate negotiations. It refers to an international meeting in the Japanese city of Kyoto in 1997, when governments agreed to make cuts in their greenhouse gas emissions. The Kyoto **Protocol** affects those developed industrial countries that are responsible for creating most of the greenhouse gas emissions. (It does not include some countries, such as Russia and China.) These industrial countries have been asked to limit or reduce their greenhouse gas emissions.

## Intergovernmental Panel on Climate Change (IPCC)

The Intergovernmental Panel on Climate Change (IPCC) was established in 1988. The major activity of the IPCC is to prepare a comprehensive report of climate change every five years. It assesses the impacts of climate change and works out ways of combatting and adapting to the changes. Its scientists sift through data from many different fields of research and combine it to form one overall picture. What makes the report so authoritative is that it combines the work of many experts from a wide range of backgrounds and countries.

Overall, this would require a total cut of at least five per cent from 1990 levels by the year 2012. The individual targets range from eight per cent for the European Union and seven per cent for the USA, to a ten per cent increase for Iceland. (This means that emissions in Iceland can increase by ten per cent and still be within the agreed limits.) Although the terms were drafted in 1997, the targets do not have to be met until 2012. However, US emissions are predicted to increase by more than 20 per cent by then, which means a real cut of 27 per cent is needed to meet the US target.

Negotiations continued until 2001, when 180 governments (with the exception of the USA) finally agreed to bring the Protocol into force. Unfortunately, the rules for implementing the targets were relaxed. Many organizations, such as the World Wide Fund for Nature, feel that the Protocol is too weak to have any noticeable effect and will be difficult to police. However, it is a step in the right direction and shows that governments can reach agreement on this international problem.

*'The US, the country with the greatest output of emissions that cause global warming, would bear a heavy responsibility for casting doubt on an accord unanimously approved by the international community.'*

Dominique Voynet, French Environment Minister

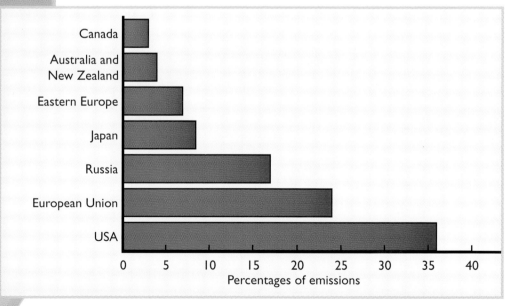

This bar chart shows the percentages of global carbon dioxide emissions from industrialized countries in 1990. The rest of the world combined contributes only two per cent of the total emissions.

## Just a fluctuation?

There is a body of scientists who do not believe that global warming is happening, or who believe that if it is happening, then it is happening at a much slower rate than people think, or is not due to humans. These scientists have interpreted the evidence in a different way. Their evidence against global warming is presented on pages 50–51.

## Problems ahead

There are now more than six billion people living in the world and each person has the potential to consume natural **resources** and energy, and to produce waste and pollution. However, not everybody uses up resources at the same rate. About 800 million people live in economically developed regions, such as Canada, the USA, Europe, Australia and Japan. They consume most of the world's resources and produce the bulk of the pollution and waste. However, there are more people who could be classed as aspiring consumers. These are the people living in fast-developing countries such as China, India, South Korea, Taiwan, Brazil, Mexico and the countries of eastern Europe. Today China has fewer cars than the US city of Los Angeles. If China's car ownership, together with oil consumption, were to match that of the USA, it would need 80 million barrels of oil per day. This is more than the world's 1996 oil output of 64 million barrels of oil per day. When the people of these developing countries increase their purchase of consumer items, such as cars, computers and other electrical goods, there will be a surge in carbon dioxide emissions.

In the recent past, bicycles were the main form of transport in China. Today, traffic jams are commonplace as the Chinese replace their bicycles with cars.

# A greenhouse world

## The greenhouse effect

The **greenhouse effect** is a natural process that keeps the Earth at a temperature that is suitable for life. It is created by gases in the **atmosphere** that absorb heat. Without the greenhouse effect, the surface of the Earth would be about 30 degrees Celsius cooler than it is today. The problem is that the greenhouse effect is getting stronger.

## The atmosphere

The atmosphere is a relatively thin layer of gases and tiny particles surrounding the Earth. The lower atmosphere, up to an altitude of about 80 km, is made up of mostly nitrogen and oxygen with smaller quantities of ten other gases. Above 80 km the quantities of the gases other than oxygen decrease, and by 150 km the atmosphere is mainly oxygen.

Closest to the ground is the troposphere, which extends to about 18 km. This is the layer that contains all the weather. Above this layer is the stratosphere, which is a calm, sunny layer. The **ozone** layer is found here. The ozone absorbs **ultraviolet radiation** from the sun. The next layer, the mesosphere, starts at about 55 km and extends to about 80 km. The outermost layer is called the thermosphere.

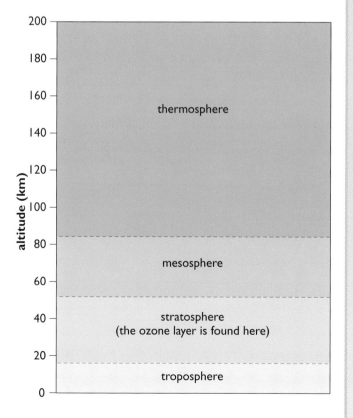

12

# Source of energy

The Sun has been radiating energy for billions of years. Its energy, in the form of **radiation**, travels as waves through space. Travelling at the phenomenal speed of 300,000 kilometres every second, the radiation reaches the upper part of the Earth's atmosphere in eight minutes. Some of this radiation is reflected back into space by clouds and by particles in the atmosphere or is absorbed by gases in the atmosphere. Some is reflected from the Earth's surface, while the rest, about half the total incoming radiation, is absorbed by the Earth's surface. This has the effect of warming the atmosphere and the ground.

As the ground gets warmer, it radiates heat back into the atmosphere. Some of it is absorbed, scattered and reflected by clouds and gases in the atmosphere and this slows down the rate at which heat is lost from the atmosphere. The rest is lost to space. The warming of the atmosphere in this way is called the greenhouse effect and the gases that absorb the radiation are called **greenhouse gases**.

## Radiation

Almost everything and everybody, including the Sun, radiates energy. The Sun emits mostly ultraviolet and visible light. Hot objects on the Earth emit mostly infrared radiation and some visible light. For example, when an electric fire is switched on it is possible to feel the infrared heat before you see the elements glowing (visible light). As the elements get hotter, they emit more light and become redder.

The diagram on the right shows how the incoming radiation from the Sun is absorbed and reflected.

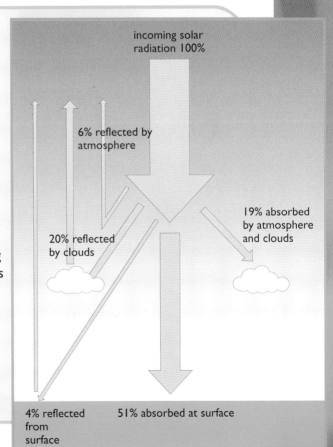

incoming solar radiation 100%

6% reflected by atmosphere

19% absorbed by atmosphere and clouds

20% reflected by clouds

4% reflected from surface

51% absorbed at surface

## Essential for life

The greenhouse effect is essential, for without the heat-absorbing capabilities of the greenhouse gases the Earth's temperature would be about -17°C. This is far too low to sustain life as we know it – most plants and animals would be unable to survive. Fortunately, however, the presence of gases, such as carbon dioxide, methane and water vapour, in the atmosphere means that the Earth's average temperature is about 15°C.

The ability of the atmosphere to retain heat means that the temperature range between day and night and over the year is small. The narrow range is important for living things as they cannot tolerate big changes in temperature. For example, plants stop photosynthesizing when the temperature rises above 40°C and when it falls to freezing. Mammals, too, although they can regulate their body temperature, find it difficult to live in the extremes of temperature experienced in the polar regions and in hot deserts.

## Getting warmer

Over the last couple of hundred years, human activities have led to an increase in the quantities of greenhouse gases in the atmosphere. This is known as the enhanced greenhouse effect. More heat has been trapped in the atmosphere. This has caused the average temperature of the Earth to increase by 0.6 degrees Celsius over the last 100 years. This, in turn, has led to **global warming**.

Many animals and plants find it hard to survive in very hot, dry conditions, like this Mexican scrub land.

# The greenhouse gases

There are a number of different greenhouses gases in the atmosphere, including water vapour, carbon dioxide, methane, nitrous oxide and chlorofluorocarbons (**CFC**s – see page 19). These gases differ in their concentration, in their effectiveness at trapping heat and in the length of their lifetime. Water vapour is present in huge quantities in the atmosphere and is the most effective greenhouse gas of all. However, its concentration in the atmosphere is not directly affected by human activities.

## Global warming potential

The gases differ in their effectiveness or global warming potential (GWP). Carbon dioxide is given a GWP of 1, making it easy to compare its effect with other gases. For example, a molecule of CFC-11 has a GWP of 3400. This shows that it is thousands of times more effective at absorbing heat than a molecule of carbon dioxide. So, scientists need to know both the concentration of a gas in the atmosphere and its GWP. The concentration of CFCs in the atmosphere is very small compared with carbon dioxide. But each CFC molecule is thousands of times more effective in absorbing heat.

| Greenhouse gas | Atmospheric concentration (parts per million by volume) | Rate of increase (% per year) | Global warming potential (GWP) | Lifetime (years) |
|---|---|---|---|---|
| carbon dioxide | 355 | 0.5 | 1 | 120 |
| methane | 1.72 | 0.6–0.75 | 21 | 10 |
| nitrous oxides | 0.31 | 0.2–0.3 | 206 | 132 |
| CFC-11 | 0.000255 | 4 | 3400 | 55 |
| CFC-12 | 0.000453 | 4 | 7100 | 116 |

This table lists the main greenhouse gases, their concentration in the atmosphere, the rate at which they are increasing and their global warming potential.

'There is at the moment no obvious mechanism that will slow, stop or otherwise deflect the warming, short of stabilization of the composition of the atmosphere by human action.'
George M. Woodwell, Director of the Woods Hole Research Center, USA

# Carbon dioxide

Carbon dioxide is probably the most important greenhouse gas. Before 1750 its concentration in the atmosphere was 280 parts per million (ppm). Today, that figure has risen to 355 ppm. The present carbon dioxide concentration has not been exceeded during the past 420,000 years. The current rate of increase is unprecedented during at least the past 20,000 years.

About three-quarters of the emissions of carbon dioxide due to human activities over the past 20 years comes from the burning of **fossil fuels**. Fossil fuels – coal, gas and oil – are the ancient remains of plants and animals, and they take millions of years to form. When they are burnt, they release heat together with carbon dioxide and water vapour. Fossil fuels have many uses, for example to power vehicles, heat homes and businesses and power factories. Since 1990, nearly half the total increase in global carbon dioxide emissions has come from the USA, exceeding the combined growth in emissions from China, India, Africa and Latin America. By 1997, the USA was responsible for about one-fifth of total global greenhouse gas emissions.

The remaining emissions of carbon dioxide come from changes in land use, especially **deforestation**. Over the last 30 years, deforestation has steadily increased. The burning of forests, especially rainforests, adds carbon dioxide to the atmosphere, as does the burning of firewood.

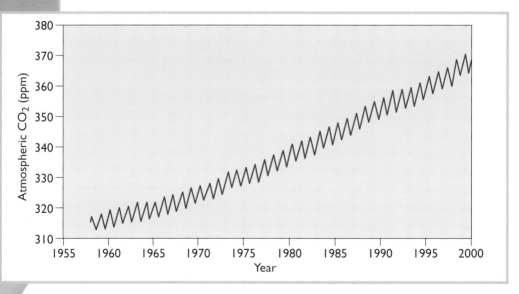

This graph shows the rise in atmospheric carbon dioxide levels over the last forty years, recorded at a scientific monitoring station in Hawaii, in the Pacific.

**Respiration** in living organisms produces carbon dioxide. Some of the carbon dioxide is taken up by plants when they **photosynthesize** (see panel). Large areas of forests are known as **carbon sinks** because of the quantity of carbon dioxide that they absorb. However, more carbon dioxide is entering the atmosphere from natural and artificial sources than can be taken up by plants and other carbon sinks. The result is that the level of carbon dioxide is increasing. This is made worse by the fact that huge areas of forests are being cleared, which is further reducing the amount of photosynthesis that can take place.

## The carbon cycle

All living organisms contain the element carbon. This carbon comes from and is returned to the atmosphere. Plants and certain micro-organisms take in carbon dioxide during photosynthesis. Carbon dioxide and water, in the presence of light, are used to make carbohydrates, such as glucose, sucrose and starch. Carbohydrates are used by plants to fuel growth. Oxygen is a bi-product. When plants, animals and micro-organisms respire, they release carbon dioxide back into the air. When they die, their remains are decomposed by organisms such as fungi and bacteria and this releases carbon dioxide, too.

The oceans have a separate carbon cycle. Carbon dioxide dissolves in seawater and is taken up by the plant plankton for photosynthesis. Some of the carbon dioxide becomes incorporated into the shells of marine organisms, such as molluscs. When these animals die, they sink to the sea floor where the carbon is locked up in sediments for millions of years. Some of these sediments form rocks, such as limestone, while others may turn into oil and gas over millions of years.

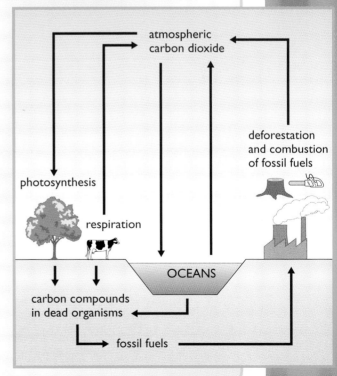

## Methane

Methane is produced by bacteria that live in swamps, rice paddies and landfill sites (large holes in the ground where rubbish is buried). In recent decades, more land has been used for rice farming and far more landfill sites have been created. There are also methane-producing bacteria in the stomachs of **ruminant** animals, such as cows and sheep. These bacteria digest the grass that the cow eats. One of the waste products is methane. Each day a belching cow may release up to 200 litres of methane. Currently, the number of cattle in the world is on the increase.

A large amount of organic matter, such as garden waste, soil, food and animal waste, gets dumped at landfill sites. As the materials rot, they release methane gas.

## Nitrous oxide

Nitrous oxide is released when fossil fuels are burnt. It is also released by bacteria that convert nitrate in the soil into nitrous oxide. There has been an increase in the area of land under cultivation and the use of nitrate fertilizers to increase crop growth. Both these factors have led to an increase in the release of nitrous oxides.

# CFCs

CFCs (chlorofluorocarbons) are synthetic chemicals that were used as coolants in refrigerators and freezers, as propellants in aerosols and in expanded polystyrene foam. The use of CFCs has contributed to two major environmental problems – damage to the ozone layer and global warming. CFCs move up into the stratosphere where they destroy ozone molecules in the ozone layer. Ozone is essential as it absorbs harmful ultraviolet light before it reaches the ground. The thinning of the ozone layer has led to increasing amounts of ultraviolet light reaching the ground. This increases the risk of people developing skin cancer and eye problems.

However, CFCs do not just destroy ozone. They are potent greenhouse gases. The use of CFCs has now been banned in most countries and they have been replaced by other chemicals. However, their lifespan is long and their effect is still being felt. It is important to remember that ozone damage and global warming are two serious, but separate, environmental problems.

To prevent the release of CFCs into the atmosphere, the coolants in fridges and freezers must be removed when the appliances are no longer needed.

# Weather watch

It is important to monitor changes in the **atmosphere** to determine the effects of **global warming**. All forms of weather data are important, including looking at changes in patterns of rainfall and temperature, changes in ocean currents, and cloud formation. Some of this data is collected using observers at traditional weather stations, but nowadays much is collected by **satellites**.

## Weather stations

There are more than 10,000 land-based weather stations around the world, some on the roofs of buildings, others on remote islands and mountain tops. Some are staffed, but most are automatic. These weather stations collect information every three hours on rainfall, temperature, wind direction and speed, and humidity (the amount of moisture in the air). This data is passed on to the World Meteorological Organization's network of meteorology centres (see panel).

## Satellite monitoring

Weather satellites were first used in 1960. Today, there are many weather satellites operated by the USA, the European Space Agency, Japan and Russia. Geostationary satellites orbit the Earth 35,900 kilometres above the Equator. These satellites can stay above the same point on the ground all the time. Polar-orbiting satellites circle the Earth from pole to pole at a lower altitude of 1000 kilometres. This means they can provide a more detailed picture of a smaller area.

A **radiosonde** is a helium-filled balloon that is used to monitor conditions high in the atmosphere. It rises into the air trailing a long line to which instruments are attached. The automatic instruments record temperature, air pressure, wind speed and humidity up to altitudes of 20,000 metres. The data is transmitted by radio to weather stations.

# World Meteorological Organization (WMO)

The WMO was created in 1951 as a specialized agency of the United Nations. It co-ordinates global scientific activity, including weather prediction, air pollution research, **climate** change related activities, **ozone** layer depletion studies and tropical storm forecasting. One of its most important roles is the production of accurate weather information, which can be used for public, private and commercial use by groups including the international airline and shipping industries. This is achieved through a programme called World Weather Watch. Information comes from 10,000 land observation stations, 7000 weather ships and 300 automatic weather stations on moored and drifting ocean buoys. The information is transmitted by satellite to three world, 35 regional and 183 national meteorological centres, which co-operate with each other in preparing weather analyses and forecasts.

Some satellites carry instruments called radiometers or **thermal** infrared (light that is beyond the visible spectrum) scanners. A hot object will emit infrared light – the hotter the object the more infrared they emit. The radiometers have sensors that can record infrared radiation. They can show variations in the temperatures of clouds, land, oceans and buildings. Radiometers are useful for tracking clouds, ocean currents, forest fires and thermal pollution.

The American National Oceanic and Atmospheric Administration (NOAA) has polar-orbiting satellites that scan the atmosphere twice daily from an altitude of 854 kilometres. They carry special radiometers that are good at showing up cloud patterns.

Satellites can also be used to monitor changes in cloud positions. Recordings are made every 30 minutes and this information can be used to trace wind speed and direction.

This satellite photograph shows Hurricane Mitch (the white area on the left) in the Atlantic Ocean moving towards Central America in 1999.

# Historical clues

Historical data are important, too. For example, when ice forms, it traps bubbles of air. The ice sheets in the polar regions have built up over thousands of years. By drilling a core through the ice, scientists can sample air bubbles from different time periods and analyse their composition, especially the carbon dioxide concentration. This is like using a corer to remove the core from an apple, where the core is removed, but the rest of the apple is left intact. Scientists can also learn about past climates by studying pollen, tree rings and coral. Pollen is preserved in peat deposits. Just like ice cores, scientists can take a core of peat dating back hundreds, often thousands of years. By identifying the pollen in the peat, they can work out which plants were living at the time and the type of conditions they required. When a tree is cut down, it is possible to see the growth rings. Each year a tree produces a growth or annual ring. The width of the ring gives scientists clues about the weather. For example, trees produce less growth in hot, dry years. Some types of coral grow very slowly and have long lifespans. Marine scientists studying coral can obtain information about conditions in the oceans over hundreds of years.

# Making predictions

Making predictions about the effects of global warming, and just how hot it will become, is incredibly difficult. Many organizations input meteorological data into computer programs. This information is used

Scientists drill a core from the ice sheet in Antarctica. The spiral apparatus is twisted down and around until it reaches solid ground. It is then pulled out carrying with it a sample of the ice.

to carry out mathematical calculations that predict overall changes to the world **climate**. A **simulation** may run for many months before it is complete. Once complete it may be run again with increasing concentrations of **greenhouse gases** to estimate the effects that these changes could cause. As more data is collected, it is fed into the simulations making them more accurate and reliable. However, even the most complex computer models are nowhere near as complex as the real world. Small-scale processes, such as cloud formation, can only be included by using simplified representations. This leads to possible errors in the final predictions.

## Feedback mechanisms

If global temperatures rise further, it is possible that there will be processes set into action that reverse the change. This is called negative feedback. It is a bit like the central-heating system in a house. When room temperatures rise, the increase is detected by the thermostat, which switches off heaters and radiators to allow the temperature to fall.

One type of negative feedback could be cloud cover. Water evaporates from surfaces and rises into the atmosphere where it cools. It **condenses** to form clouds. As the temperature increases there will be an increase in evaporation and more water will condense to form clouds. More cloud cover could reflect more of the incoming **radiation** and reduce the amount of heat absorbed by the Earth's surface.

But the opposite could happen. The increased amount of evaporation could mean there is more water vapour in the atmosphere and water vapour is a greenhouse gas. This could lead to a further increase in temperature. This is called positive feedback – as something increases, it causes change, which results in even greater increases.

As described here, an increase in water vapour could have one of two possible effects. One outcome could be that the water vapour helps to cool the Earth; the other is that it helps to warm up the Earth. Unfortunately at the moment, scientists have no way of knowing which of these scenarios will be correct.

Temperature, too, could have a positive feedback effect on plants. As temperatures increase, the chemical reactions that take place inside the plant increase, too. If plants start to respire more quickly, they produce more carbon dioxide. More carbon dioxide will increase the greenhouse effect and cause temperatures to rise.

# Climatic consequences

A changing **climate** is a global problem. It will not just affect one part of the world – it will affect everybody and everything. Some of the changes are already underway. Most scientists agree that temperatures will rise, but the amount by which they will rise and how quickly is still being debated. In 2001, the **IPCC** published its latest assessment in which it warns that **global warming** is occurring more rapidly than previously believed and that most of the warming observed over the last 50 years is due to human activities. Its chief findings include:

- the average global surface temperature is projected to rise by between 1.4 and 5.8 degrees Celsius by 2100
- the 1990s was the warmest decade and 1998 the warmest year since global temperature observations began in 1861
- global sea level in the past century has risen at a rate ten times faster than during any time over the last 3000 years and it is projected to rise by about 8 to 72 centimetres between 1990 and 2100
- snow cover and the extent of sea-ice in the northern hemisphere are projected to decrease further.

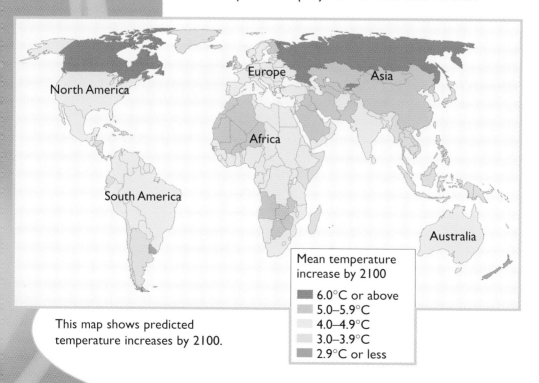

This map shows predicted temperature increases by 2100.

Mean temperature increase by 2100

- 6.0°C or above
- 5.0–5.9°C
- 4.0–4.9°C
- 3.0–3.9°C
- 2.9°C or less

*'The drastic temperature increase, and increasing potential for floods, droughts and other impacts predicted by the IPCC represent an unprecedented consensus among hundreds of climate change experts from all over the world. This new benchmark for what we know about global warming makes it evermore clear that the world faces an even more severe challenge from global warming than the previous IPCC report in 1995 suggested.'*

Dr Susanne Moser, Staff Scientist
at the Union of Concerned Scientists

## Unequal rises

As the Earth warms up, the various regions of the world will warm up by different amounts. Although the average rise is predicted at between 1.4 and 5.8 degrees Celsius, some places could have much greater rises. The central regions of Asia such as Kazakhstan, Mongolia and Uzbekistan already experience very hot summers when temperatures exceed 40°C. Summer droughts have become far more common. Scientists predict that central Asian countries could experience a warming of more than 6 degrees Celsius by 2100. In contrast, the rise in temperature in Britain, Ireland, New Zealand, Chile, Uruguay and Argentina could be 3 degrees Celsius or less. Many of the countries that face the greatest rises are economically poor and produce the smallest amounts of **greenhouse gases**.

Disrupted weather patterns have been experienced in Central Mongolia. Recently the area has suffered its worst drought in 60 years, followed by the harshest winter in 30 years. In winter 2000, 1.8 million domestic animals froze to death.

## Changing rainfall patterns

The global average water vapour concentration and **precipitation** are expected to increase during the course of the 21st century. As the Earth warms up, there will be greater evaporation. This will lead to a rise in moisture in the atmosphere and more rainfall. This will increase average global precipitation.

Not all places will experience the same changes. By the second half of the 21st century, it is likely that precipitation will have increased over northern mid- to high latitudes and Antarctica in winter. Severe rainstorms are likely to become more frequent. There may be a greater variation in precipitation from year to year. In contrast, some regions could experience an overall decrease in soil moisture. There would be less evaporation and lower rainfall. This could create desert-like conditions in these regions.

## Shifting climates

The climate is one factor that determines the type of vegetation in an area. Global warming will cause changes in the vegetation. The largest changes are expected to occur at the poles, where there could be the greatest increases in temperature.

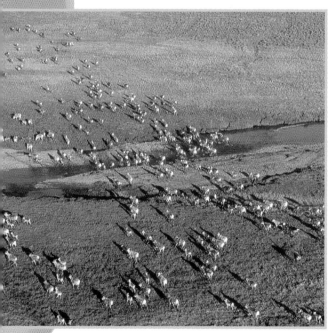

It is likely that the coniferous forests that cover much of northern Canada and Siberia will extend northwards replacing the **tundra**. Tundra is low-growing boggy vegetation, which is adapted to the short growing season. A few metres below ground level the soil is permanently frozen. This is called **permafrost**. As the temperatures increase, the permafrost will melt and remain unfrozen for long periods of time. This will allow trees to become established (see page 33).

A change in the climate in the Arctic will affect migratory animals, such as the caribou.

Desert regions, especially those in Africa and Australia, are likely to expand as the temperatures increase. Already these areas have experienced problems as a result of drought and overgrazing by livestock. The vegetation cover has been lost and this has affected the water cycle, leading to drought. This is called desertification.

# Dust

The amount of dust in the atmosphere could reduce some of the global warming. Scientists studying dust blowing off the Sahara Desert have found that dust particles could lessen the amount of solar warming of the Earth's surface. This means that the Earth's surface receives less warmth in areas where dust lingers in the atmosphere, and more **radiation** is reflected back into space.

# Oceanic effects

The rising global temperatures could have wide-ranging effects on the world's oceans and glaciers. This, in turn, could affect the world's climates. When liquids get warmer they expand and fill more space. This is happening with the water in the oceans. Since there is so much water, even tiny increases of temperature cause the volume of the water to expand and this is increasing sea levels all over the world. Increasing global temperatures are causing the ice of glaciers and ice sheets to melt, too. Glaciers are retreating and in the Antarctic huge slabs of ice are falling into the sea. The Antarctic ice sheet has always lost ice, but much larger slabs are coming away and the sheet is beginning to break up in places.

The estimates of sea level increases vary, but most suggest that sea level could rise by as much as 72 centimetres over the next 100 years. This may not seem much, but in some places, because of their geography, the rise could be several metres. The increasing sea level threatens low-lying land, such as Bangladesh, coral islands such as the Maldives, parts of eastern England and the Netherlands and the coastal regions of the USA. The more severe weather and increasing intensity of wind will increase the height of waves. This is likely to lead to more coastal erosion in areas where sea level is increasing.

## Hurricane alert

Hurricanes (also called typhoons and cyclones) are tropical storms that form over warm water. They feed on the energy of the water. The warmer the water the more energy there is, allowing a more intense storm to develop. As ocean waters get warmer, there is more likelihood of these storms developing.

# The Gulf Stream

The **temperate** climate of north-west Europe is largely due to the **Gulf Stream**. This is an ocean current carrying warm water across the Atlantic Ocean from the Gulf of Mexico. The Gulf Stream keeps north-west Europe 5 to 10 degrees Celsius warmer than it would otherwise be.

The Gulf Stream is part of an oceanic circulation that acts as a giant heating system for the region. As the warm water reaches the cooler seas between Greenland and Norway, it becomes cold and dense enough to sink below the surface. Cold, deep water currents return south towards the Equator, to be warmed again.

There is evidence that, in the past, this circulation has switched rapidly between 'on' and 'off' over a period of a few decades. This dramatically affected the climate of the region during the last Ice Age. Current climate models suggest that the climatic change over the next 100 years could cause this ocean current to be switched off, resulting in a sudden cooling for north-west Europe as the rest of the world heats up. The latest data indicates that there has been a slowing down of about 20 per cent in the flow of water.

# El Niño and La Niña

A cold current flows up the western coast of South America bringing with it waters rich in nutrients. Plankton feed on the nutrients and huge shoals of anchovy feed on the plankton. However, every three to eight years, this cold current is replaced by a warm one, which appears in late December off the South American coast. It is called 'El Niño' (which is Spanish for 'the little boy' or 'Christ-child'). The arrival of **El Niño** spells disaster for Peruvian anchovy fishermen until the normal cold water current returns. Another change, called La Niña ('the little girl'), is the appearance of abnormally cold ocean surface temperatures in the Equatorial Pacific.

Normally, the cold water current flows north from the Southern Ocean along the west coast of South America. Then it flows west along the Equator where it is heated by the sun. This means that the western Pacific Ocean near Australia and Indonesia is 3 to 8 degrees Celsius warmer than the eastern part.

However, during an El Niño the weather patterns and ocean currents change. Warmer waters develop in the eastern Pacific and air temperatures rise by 2 to 8 degrees Celsius. Storm clouds build up bringing heavy rains to the western side of South America. On the other side of the ocean, around Northern Australia and Indonesia, the seas cool and rainfall is lower.

Recently, the frequency of El Niño has increased. El Niño has been returning within two to three years of the last one, or sometimes continued for more than a year. The longest El Niño of the 20th century persisted from 1991 to 1995, and was rapidly succeeded by the most intense El Niño of the 20th century, which occurred in the period 1997–98. It affected the western tropical Pacific where it caused widespread drought. In Indonesia the rainfall was 50 per cent below normal. Drought affected many areas and huge fires raged across the country covering an area in excess of ten million hectares on the islands of Borneo and Sumatra. Half of this land was rainforest. These huge fires lasted months and created an atmospheric haze over the region for more than a year. The haze cut out sunlight, and daytime temperatures were as much as 6 degrees Celsius below normal. Nobody can be certain whether the increasing frequency and strength of El Niños is connected to global warming. Research is underway to determine if there is a link.

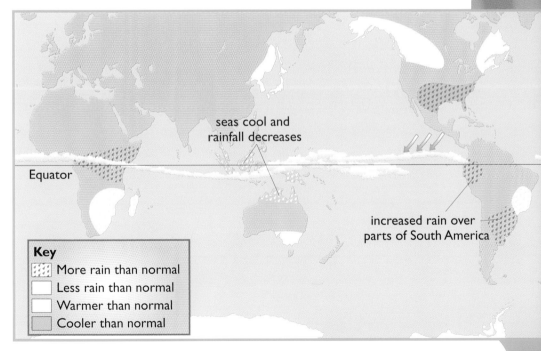

seas cool and
rainfall decreases

Equator

increased rain over
parts of South America

Key
More rain than normal
Less rain than normal
Warmer than normal
Cooler than normal

This map shows the regions affected by El Niño. The western Pacific experiences periods of drought, while in South America there is increased rainfall.

The sea level has risen around the Maldive Islands in the Indian Ocean. The image on the left was taken five years before the one on the right. In that time, much of the beach has disappeared.

## Problems for islands and coastal zones

Many coral islands lie just a metre or so above sea level. Low-lying islands, such as the Maldives, Seychelles and various Pacific islands, could disappear completely if sea levels rise further. Already the damage can be seen. Some sandy beaches have disappeared under the sea. Other beaches have to be protected by concrete blocks and other erosion control measures. In addition, the warming of the seas is causing coral **bleaching** (see page 34). Within a few years of coral bleaching, the fish decline in number. The local people depend on the seas for much of their food, so healthy fish stocks are important. Tourism is also important and the loss of beaches and the damage to coral reefs are having an adverse effect on the numbers of tourists who visit. Unfortunately there is nothing these nations can do to stop the seas from rising. They can only raise public awareness and hope that the developed countries will cut their carbon dioxide emissions.

The sea level is rising more rapidly along some coasts than others, for example along the Atlantic coasts of the USA and Brazil. Studies by the US Environmental Protection Agency estimate that along the Gulf and Atlantic coasts, a 30-centimetre. rise in sea level could occur as soon as 2025.

Over the next century, a 60-centimetre rise is most likely, but a 120-centimetre rise is possible and the sea level will probably continue to rise for several centuries, even if global temperatures were to stop rising.

Rising sea levels flood wetlands and other low-lying lands, erode beaches and increase the salinity (amount of salt present) of rivers and groundwater. This could have an adverse effect on farming, as most crop plants will not grow in salty soil. Coastal marshes and swamps are particularly vulnerable to rising sea levels because they are barely a metre or so above the sea. As the sea rises, new wetlands could form inland as previously dry areas are flooded by the higher water levels. However, the area of newly created wetlands will be much smaller than the area of wetlands that are lost.

## Are glaciers retreating?

In 2000, the Mendenhall Glacier in Alaska retreated by 100 metres revealing land that had been hidden under the ice for centuries. Since the 1930s this glacier has lost almost a kilometre of its length. Glaciologist Keith Echelmeyer is surveying 90 glaciers in Alaska and neighbouring areas to determine if they are changing. The results from the first eight years have shown that most of the glaciers are shrinking rapidly and may not survive this century. Once mapped, the results are compared with aerial photographs taken 50 years ago by the US geological survey. On average these glaciers are thinning by up to 1.5 metres per year. A few are thinning by up to 3 metres per year. This means that glaciers which are only 200 metres thick may last less than 100 years, especially as the rate of thinning speeds up as the glacier gets thinner. However, a shrinking glacier is not necessarily a sign of global warming, as glaciers are known to go through cycles of thickening and thinning. Some glaciers have been seen to go through decades of thinning while neighbouring ones get thicker. It is too early to tell if these changes are the beginning of a trend or just a blip.

## Long-term changes

The increases in the average global surface temperatures and the rising sea levels caused by the **thermal** expansion of the oceans are projected to continue for hundreds of years even if the amount of **greenhouse gases** are stabilized. This is due to the long period of time that greenhouse gases remain in the atmosphere and the time it takes deep oceans to adjust to climate change. The ice sheets will also continue to melt for hundreds, even thousands of years after climates have been stabilized.

31

# Biological changes

Plants and animals often adapt to live in one particular type of habitat. If this changes, they are forced to adapt once more or to move to somewhere more favourable. This means that **global warming** could result in a fall in **biodiversity**. As global temperatures rise there will be winners and losers. Those species that cannot tolerate any change in their environment may become extinct. Animals and plants that are naturally adaptable will be best placed to take advantage of any change in **climate**. Many of the plants and animals that we see in our towns and cities once lived in forests or grasslands. They were adaptable enough to take advantage of the new habitats being created in urban areas. It is these types of animals and plants that will be most able to adapt to changing climatic conditions.

## Most at risk

The term 'range' is used to describe the area in which a particular plant species can be found growing. Some species have a very limited range and they are only found in a few specific places. Other species are more tolerant and can be found growing in a greater range of places. The species most at risk are those that are living at the edge of their range. These species are vulnerable since they are already existing under conditions which may not

Semi-arid scrub, such as this in the Northern Territories of Australia, is found around desert areas and is most at risk from climate changes.

be ideal, perhaps too hot in summer or too cold in winter. Any change, however small, may be sufficient to tip the balance and cause them to become extinct locally. Few plants and animals are found in the semi-arid areas around hot deserts. Most cannot survive the desert conditions, but are able to live in places where there is slightly more water. Any extension of the desert regions will cause them to disappear. There is a huge expanse of semi-arid grassland in the central regions of Australia. A decrease in the already low rainfall would cause many plants to die.

## Effects on forests

The current distribution of different types of forest is mostly determined by climate. A change in the climate could have an impact on the composition and health of forests. The plants and animals that live in the forests are dependent upon each other. The loss of certain tree species would affect the animal species that depend on them.

Warmer temperatures and changes in soil moisture levels may cause the disappearance of many tree species. Forests in New England, USA, and in Canada may lose some familiar eastern forest species such as the sugar maple. This would reduce the impact of the autumn colours and damage the maple-sugar producing industry. In the Pacific Northwest and California, the forests dominated by Douglas fir and ponderosa pine could be replaced with open grasslands and scrub. The northerly forests, the **boreal** forests of Canada and Siberia, may extend northwards, replacing the **tundra**.

Within the next 100 years, many forest species may be forced to migrate between 200 and 400 kilometres in the direction of the poles. Forest species have migrated this far in the past, but over thousands of years, not decades. It is more likely that there will be a loss of forest biodiversity and some species may become extinct. However, new species may become established.

Autumn colours in Canada and the USA are popular with tourists. The colours form when the trees break down the green pigment in their leaves, leaving substances that turn the leaves red and orange.

# Mountains

The warming temperatures will probably cause a shift in the distribution of vegetation to higher altitudes. Animals and plants that are currently only found at the higher altitudes may become extinct due to the disappearance of their habitat. Leisure activities, such as skiing, are likely to be disrupted and this could have an adverse effect on the economies of some mountain regions.

> 'Whereas in the past human impacts were local, reversible, and escapable through migration, they are now typically global, irreversible, and inescapable.'
>
> Paul Ehrlich

# Coral bleaching

Coral reefs are found in tropical seas where there is clean, clear unpolluted water. A sudden change in temperature of just one degree Celsius can have devastating effects. Corals are animals that are related to sea anemones. They build a limestone skeleton around their soft bodies. Corals have tiny algae living in their cells.

A large area of bleached stagshorn coral in the Great Barrier Reef, Australia. As much as 60 per cent of the coral forming the Great Barrier Reef may have been affected by bleaching.

The algae **photosynthesize** and supply the coral with food. In return the algae gain shelter. This arrangement where both partners gain is known as a symbiotic or mutualistic relationship. The algae also give the corals their colour. If the temperature changes, **bleaching** occurs as the corals lose their algae and become white. Without their algae they do not grow as well. If the coral suffers a setback, the rest of the food chain is affected. In recent years, bleaching has been reported on many coral reefs. In 1998, reefs around the Maldives were bleached and this has severely affected fish stocks and tourism. In many cases, the change in water temperature was caused by severe **El Niño** and La Niña events (see pages 28–29).

# Crops

Although total global food production is not expected to change substantially, there could be dramatic regional changes. Factors such as the length of growing season, the timing of the last frosts and the amount of rainfall all affect the type of crops that can be grown. As a result of global warming, the growing season in the more northerly and southerly latitudes may get longer and this will allow different crops to be grown. Sunflowers are a common sight in southern Europe, but these crops could be grown in northern Europe. Maize, too, could be grown. At present it is grown as a fodder crop for animals, but more varieties of frost-sensitive maize could be grown more widely.

However, these changes could also leave major grain-growing regions, such as the North Amercian prairies and steppes in Russia, with long dry summers and frequent droughts. The variety of crops that can be grown in a region is predicted to decline and this could lead to greater dependence on one or two crops. Developed countries may be able to adapt to these circumstances. Developing countries that currently struggle to produce healthy harvests are likely to suffer even more.

A drop in productivity of the main cereal-producing areas would have major consequences on the global economy. The summer of 1988 in North America was marked by a heatwave and drought. The cereal crop fell by 30 per cent and this affected the global price of cereals and caused shortages. With global warming, losses in the production of cereal crops are expected in high production areas, such as southern Europe, southern USA and western Australia. This could be offset by a limited warming in areas further north and south where the climate could be more favourable for these crops. However, these areas do not have the fertile soils characteristic of the current cereal growing regions.

# Pests, disease and human health

The changing climate will also affect pest and disease-causing species. This means that rising temperatures are likely to have a considerable effect on human health.

## Crop pests

As the climate warms up, it is expected that the number and types of pests in a particular region will increase. The locust is a major pest. Huge swarms of locusts regularly destroy crops in Africa. At the moment their distribution is limited by temperature. If temperatures increase, they will move further north and south.

## Mosquitoes

The *Anopheles* mosquito is a carrier of the malarial **parasite**. People become infected when they are bitten by a female mosquito carrying the parasite. **Malaria** is a major disease in the tropics, killing millions of people each year. There are drugs to treat malaria, but they are not always successful.

Prevention of malaria is far more important. People visiting malarial areas can take medicines that prevent the parasite from infecting their blood. In addition, mosquito netting over beds and insect sprays can prevent the mosquito from biting. Stagnant pools where the mosquitoes breed can be sprayed with insecticide.

Currently, just under half of the world's population lives within the malarial zone. The mosquito's range is restricted by low temperatures since frosts will kill them. As climates get warmer, however, there will be fewer frosts and heavier rainfall, allowing the mosquito to extend its range beyond the tropics. Often mountainous areas in the tropics are free of mosquitoes, but it has been reported that mosquitoes are being seen at higher altitudes.

It is estimated that the expansion of the mosquito's range will cause an extra 50 to 80 million cases of malaria worldwide each year and 60 per cent of the world's population will live in the malaria zone. Mosquitoes are also carriers of dengue fever, yellow fever and encephalitis. These diseases, too, are on the increase.

# Health hazards

As well as the increasing incidence of diseases such as malaria caused by global warming, there are likely to be other problems associated with extremes of weather. Hot summers could increase the number of deaths from heat stress. For example, in 1995, a heatwave hit Chicago and more than 450 people died.

An increase in the frequency and intensity of extreme weather events, such as flood and drought, will also cause more deaths. As well as people dying during the weather event, there will be deaths afterwards. Flooding, for example, can contaminate water supplies allowing diseases such as cholera and typhoid to spread through the population. Most developed countries are reporting a rise in the incidence of hay fever, asthma and allergies. Global warming could make this worse.

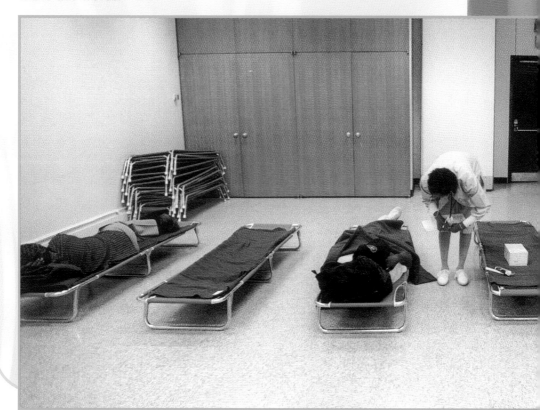

In the summer of 1995, 450 people died in Chicago, USA during a heatwave. The city set up air-conditioned 'cooling centres', like the one shown here, where people suffering from heat exhaustion could be treated.

# Combating the changes

If nothing is done to limit emissions, it is predicted that by 2100 the concentration of carbon dioxide in the **atmosphere** could be two to three times higher than the current levels. This problem has to be tackled on a global scale. There are three main approaches:

- reducing the quantity of **greenhouse gas** emissions, especially carbon dioxide, by cutting back on the use of **fossil fuels**. The fuels must be used more efficiently by applying new technology and developing new energy-saving devices
- increasing the use of **renewable** energy sources
- stopping **deforestation** and establishing a global programme of replanting trees.

## Setting limits

One way to reduce greenhouse gas emissions is to set international limits that are enforced by all countries. As described on page 10, the Kyoto **Protocol** is attempting to set legal limits to greenhouse gas emissions by the industrialized nations of the world. The ultimate objective is to stabilize concentrations of greenhouse gases in the atmosphere at the levels that existed in 1990, to avoid dangerous **climate** change.

## Fair play for all

Aubrey Meyer is a professional musician who has put forward a plan to cut global greenhouse gas emissions. His plan has won the backing of many countries, including China and the European Union. Currently the USA emits 5.2 tonnes of carbon per person per year, the UK emits 2.6 tonnes, while India emits only 0.2 tonnes. Meyer has worked out that the emissions need to be cut to just 0.4 tonnes of carbon per person per year. This means that the USA has to cut its emissions by 90 per cent while India can double its emissions. Obviously this is impossible for some countries, such as the USA, without a major change in lifestyle and economy. So, countries are allowed to buy and sell their allowances. Developing countries with their low emissions will be able to trade and earn valuable income. This can be used to improve their standards of living and to pay for energy-saving technology that will keep emissions low.

People in the developed world will have to change their lifestyles if global resources are to be used fairly.

## Cutting back on fossil fuels

Fossil fuels are the main source of carbon dioxide. These fuels are burnt in power stations to generate electricity, which is used by industry and homes. The massive rise in the number of vehicles on the roads and planes in the sky has increased the use of oil in the form of petrol and diesel. All fossil fuels contain carbon, though the proportion of carbon varies. When they are burnt, they release carbon dioxide and carbon monoxide. In the European Union, the energy industries are responsible for 28 per cent of greenhouse gas emissions, the majority of which is carbon dioxide. In the UK, power stations are the biggest single source of carbon dioxide, accounting for 26 per cent of emissions in 1998. Transport is responsible for a further 22 per cent.

In recent years, the use of coal in power stations has decreased as many have switched to oil and gas. Gas burns more cleanly and efficiently than coal. It releases just half as much carbon and less than one-thousandth of the sulphur dioxide (which produces acid rain) per unit of energy. This change will help many countries reduce their carbon emissions in the short term. In addition, the efficiency with which the fossil fuels are used has improved. However, the long-term answer is to reduce global dependence on all fossil fuels.

# Energy efficiency

When energy is converted from one form to another, there is loss of useful energy in the form of heat. No energy conversion is 100 per cent efficient. Car engines are about 25 per cent efficient, while **turbines** in power stations work at 25 to 30 per cent efficiency. The rest is converted to heat energy, most of which is unwanted and represents a waste. The key is to make the conversion process as efficient as possible.

A small, local power station is more efficient than a large, central power station. There are huge energy losses when electricity is transferred along power lines to sub-stations and then to buildings. A local power station based on gas turbines can be twice as efficient as taking electricity from a huge **national grid**. In the future, local power networks supplied with electricity generated by different sources could become much more commonplace.

The latest turbines for generating electricity are far more efficient than their predecessors. The combined cycle-gas turbine operates at up to 60 per cent efficiency, nearly twice that of any other turbine.

This can be combined with devices that make use of the waste heat to warm buildings, increasing the efficiency to 90 per cent. Energy can be saved in buildings, too, which can be fitted with energy-saving lighting and heating devices. Walls and roof spaces can be insulated to reduce heat loss and windows can be fitted with double or triple glazing.

People can help by choosing to use electricity generated from renewable sources. They can fit solar panels to make use of the free energy from the Sun. They can choose to make more use of public transport, to walk or to cycle rather than take the car. Energy can be saved in the home by fitting energy-efficient light bulbs and ensuring that lights and electrical equipment are switched off when not in use.

> 'It is generally cheaper today to save fuel than to burn it. Avoiding pollution by not burning the fuel can be achieved, not at a cost – but at a profit.'
>
> Dr Amory Lovings, Director
> of Research, Rocky Mountain Institute

# Renewable energy sources

Renewable energy sources such as wind, solar and tidal power have the advantage of not emitting greenhouse gases or using a resource that cannot be replaced. A switch to renewable energy offers other benefits, including a decrease in the dependence on one fuel source – fossil fuels – and a greater diversity of energy sources. A shift to renewable energy sources is essential if countries are to meet their targets for the Kyoto Protocol. For example, the European Union is aiming to generate 22 per cent of electricity from renewable sources. Water, wind and solar energy are the most developed renewable energy sources.

## Wind power

The amount of electricity generated by wind power globally has been growing at 30 per cent per year and now generates the equivalent of 20 coal-powered power stations. Europe is leading the way on wind power, with 70 per cent of the world's wind power generation.

This Californian windfarm is located at a pass in the mountains where there are constant winds.

The North Sea represents a huge reservoir of wind power. A study conducted by Greenpeace and the German Institute for Wind Energy found that carbon dioxide savings in Germany could reach 12 million tonnes per year by 2005 if offshore wind farms were used. If all the countries bordering the North Sea meet their wind targets by 2004, a massive 21 million tonnes of carbon dioxide could be saved. In the UK in 1999 only 2.8 per cent of electricity came from renewable sources. Of this, onshore wind farms provided approximately 9 per cent. **Hydroelectric** schemes provided 50 per cent and 34 per cent came from incineration and methane from landfill. The UK's target is to generate 10 per cent of electricity from renewable sources by 2010.

*'By tapping its vast wind resources, America can boost its electricity supply by 10 to 20 per cent without additional air pollution or emissions of global warming gases, and at the same time get affordable insurance against volatile energy prices. Some utilities are beginning to do the numbers and realize that wind energy is smart business.'*

American Wind Energy Association
executive director Randall Swisher

## Solar energy

Solar power is pollution-free, once the panels have been manufactured and are put in place. There are two types of solar panel. One is used to heat water. Heat energy in sunlight heats up water as it circulates through the panel. This water can then be used in heating. More useful are the photovoltaic panels, which absorb sunlight and use it to generate electricity. Over its lifetime a single photovoltaic cell will generate more power than an equivalent-sized piece of uranium (used in nuclear reactors), prevent the use of 14 kilograms of oil and save on greenhouse emissions by 30 kilograms of carbon dioxide.

The photovoltaic cells on the roof of this house in Switzerland absorb light and use it to generate electricity. Photovoltaic cells contain thin layers of silica, of which there is an unlimited supply.

## Pricing

At present, renewable sources are not as competitively priced as fossil fuel energy, especially the more expensive schemes such as offshore wind farms.

However, the costs are falling as the technology improves. These energy sources may become more competitive if governments remove **subsidies** on fossil fuels. Some governments have plans to tax energy that is generated using fossil fuels. This is referred to as the carbon tax. It would give electricity consumers a chance to buy electricity generated from renewable sources rather than from coal, oil or gas.

## Scrap the gas guzzlers

The numbers of cars in the world has increased rapidly, especially in developing countries. **Exhaust** fumes contain many pollutant gases, including greenhouse gases. **Catalytic converters** can remove sulphur dioxide and nitrous oxides, but they do nothing about carbon dioxide. The new generation of cars is far more environmentally friendly. Often this is in response to tough environmental emissions laws. For example, California has introduced some of the toughest laws in an attempt to clean up cities such as Los Angeles. Car manufacturers, such as Ford, General Motors and Daimler Chrysler, are producing cars with zero emissions. The state laws require two per cent of the cars sold in the state to be zero-emission vehicles, rising to eight per cent by 2003.

## Nuclear power – good or bad?

Nuclear power stations use uranium as their power source. When the uranium atom is split in nuclear fission, vast amounts of energy are released, which are used to heat water to steam. The steam turns a turbine to generate electricity. The main problem with nuclear power is the waste material – it is highly radioactive and its disposal is hazardous and expensive. However, unlike power stations that burn fossil fuels, there are no greenhouse gases. In 1999, nuclear power accounted for 20 per cent of power in the USA and 34 per cent of the electricity in the European Union. Many nuclear power stations are being shut down over worries about radioactive wastes and accidents. By 2025, it is predicted that the European figure will fall to less than nine per cent. To prevent a rise in greenhouse gas emissions, the nuclear power must be replaced by another source that does not emit greenhouse gases, or electricity demand must be reduced. It is unlikely that sufficient alternatives will be in place in time. Europe has to look carefully at the future of nuclear power and if its main priority is to reduce greenhouse gases then the nuclear option has to be kept open. It is possible that new nuclear power stations, with modern control systems, will have to be built. What is worse – the threat of a nuclear accident or disrupted weather patterns, drought and floods caused by global warming?

This car has solar panels on its roof which convert
sunlight into additional power to supplement its battery.

In the future, more cars could be powered by hybrid diesel-electric
engines and **fuel cells**, which would help motorists to halve their
greenhouse gas emissions. Hybrid cars have both a battery that provides
electricity and a conventional internal combustion engine. Some of the
time they run using the conventional engine and the rest of the time on
the battery. This boosts the distance they travel on a litre of petrol
considerably and cuts down the greenhouse gas emissions.

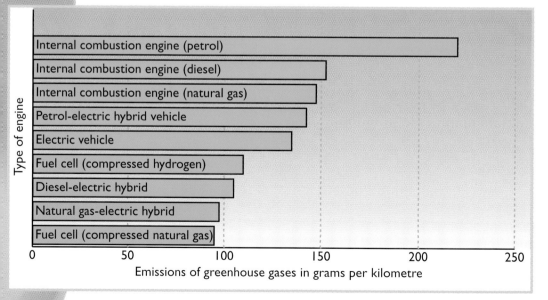

This table shows the emissions of different types of engines.
Note that some types of internal combustion engine have
much lower emissions than others.

Emissions can be cut further by using an engine powered by hydrogen gas. Hydrogen has a lot of potential. Currently, hydrogen is produced using natural gas, but soon it will be economic to produce it by electrolysis. When an electric current is passed through water it splits the water molecule into hydrogen and oxygen gases, which can be collected. At the moment, the electricity would probably be supplied by a power station using fossil fuel. But if the electricity was generated from a renewable source, the greenhouse gas emissions would be zero.

Another alternative is an engine powered by a fuel cell running on compressed natural gas or hydrogen. A fuel cell is a bit like a battery. Within the fuel cell, oxygen and hydrogen are combined to produce electricity. The only waste material is water. These systems were developed by the space programme, but have great potential, especially for use in buildings and electric cars.

> 'According to our calculations in our study, there is considerable greenhouse gas benefit by changing to hybrid or fuel cell vehicles in the near future.'
>
> Jurgen Louis, researcher for the oil company, Shell

# Technology

Technology is an important component in the efforts to reduce greenhouse gas emissions. With growing populations, the role of climate-friendly technology will become even more critical. Technological advances in power generation and the development of renewable sources of energy are needed. One of the major concerns is that the less developed countries will not be able to afford the technology to help them reduce their greenhouse gas emissions. As a result, the Kyoto Protocol has made provisions for the industrial countries to provide technological and financial support to the developing countries. The Climate Technology Initiative (CTI) is a voluntary, multilateral co-operative programme to help support the implementation of the United Nations Framework Convention on Climate Change. The CTI promotes national and international policies that help the transfer of environmentally appropriate technologies.

> 'Those countries that address climate change earliest will dominate the massive new energy technology markets of the new century and create millions of jobs in the process.'
>
> Chris Flavin, Worldwatch Institute in Washington, DC

# The role of forests

Plants take in carbon dioxide during **photosynthesis** and release carbon dioxide during **respiration**. They are in equilibrium with the atmosphere because they take and release similar amounts. Globally plants take in and release 60 billion tonnes of carbon each year. These exchanges of carbon are large, dwarfing the 6.5 billion tonnes released by burning fossil fuels.

Most of the photosynthesis and respiration is carried out by ecosystems that produce woody material, such as forests. A newly planted forest with young trees will not be in equilibrium with the atmosphere. These trees are growing and laying down new wood so they will take in more carbon dioxide than they give out. For this reason, young forests are referred to as **carbon sinks** as they take in far more carbon than they release. The carbon is eventually released when the trees die and decay or when the trees are burnt for fuel.

Broadscale clearing of native tree species in this Australian forest will decrease absorption of carbon dioxide.

# Deforestation

Deforestation is second only to fossil fuels as a contributor to global warming. Since the beginning of industrialization, the loss of forests is believed to account for between a third and a half of all carbon dioxide released into the atmosphere. Deforestation is taking place all over the world. The best known deforestation is that of the tropical rainforests. However, coniferous forests in Russia and North America are also being cleared. Trees are felled for fuel in many parts of Africa, India and South-East Asia. Unfortunately, old forests are being cleared at an increasing rate, releasing vast amounts of previously locked up carbon into the atmosphere. Young forests would have to be grown for hundreds of years just to offset the carbon released from the logging of ancient forests. So, one of the easiest and most effective ways of stabilizing the carbon dioxide levels would be to halt deforestation immediately.

It is possible to increase the global uptake of carbon dioxide by planting new forests. Fast-growing plants such as willow, poplar and grasses can also be grown as a crop. These plants are allowed to grow for a few seasons, before being harvested and burnt. These renewable crops are referred to as a **biomass**. Biomass as a source of energy is described as greenhouse gas neutral. In other words, the amount of carbon dioxide taken up by the plants when they are growing equals the amount of carbon dioxide released when they are burnt.

## More carbon dioxide

Even if huge replanting programmes are carried out, it may not be enough to reduce the carbon dioxide emissions. Generally the amount of carbon dioxide taken up by photosynthesis equals that given out by respiration of living organisms. As it gets warmer these processes speed up. More carbon dioxide in the air will increase the rate at which plants take up carbon dioxide, which is a good thing. But as it gets hotter, the amount they take up levels off. At the same time, the amount of carbon dioxide released by micro-organisms in the soil increases. So, as the temperatures increase, so does the amount of carbon dioxide being released from **ecosystems**. This will be made worse by the fact that the warming could turn large areas of the Amazon rainforest into grasslands that take up less carbon dioxide.

## Seeding the seas

It is possible that the seas could take up more carbon dioxide. Experiments in the Southern Ocean have involved fertilizing the seas with iron. Iron, an essential nutrient, was found to be in short supply in the Southern Ocean. The addition of iron boosted the growth of plant plankton. The plankton carried out more photosynthesis and so used up more of the carbon dioxide dissolved in the water. The carbon dioxide was replaced by sucking more from the air. Even if this method proves feasible, there are many problems. First, the take-up of carbon dioxide is quite small, much less than the vast amounts of carbon dioxide being produced. In addition, there is no way of knowing how an increase in the plankton could affect the marine food chains. It could trigger changes in the marine ecosystems, which could lead to increases in greenhouse gases, not decreases.

'There are still fundamental scientific questions that need to be addressed before anyone can responsibly promote iron fertilization as a climate control action.'

Dr. Kenneth H. Coale, an oceanographer

# Reducing methane and CFCs

As well as tackling carbon dioxide emissions, it is also essential to reduce the emissions of gases such as methane and to control **CFCs**. These gases have a far greater global warming potential (see page 15).

## Methane

Methane released from rotting material in landfill sites is usually allowed to escape into the atmosphere or is burnt off. However, the methane could be collected and used as a fuel. Methane releases carbon dioxide when burnt, but the use of methane as a fuel could reduce the quantity of fossil fuels being used.

## Rice

Young rice plants are planted in flooded fields called paddies. The waterlogged soils contain micro-organisms which release methane. In recent years, the area of land used to grow rice has increased, and this has resulted in an increase in the production of methane. More research is needed to learn about how the methane is released, and how the irrigation and cultivation of the rice affects the formation of methane. One way forward may be to use higher-yielding and faster-maturing varieties of rice, in order to get the same amount of rice in a shorter time from less land. However, faster-yielding crops may persuade more farmers to grow several crops each year. The yield would be increased, but the paddy fields would remain flooded for longer each year and methane emissions could increase rather than decrease. Another approach may be to develop new strains of rice that have a higher ratio of grain to non-grain, so there is less waste to be left to decay in the fields.

## Cattle diets

Cattle are another source of methane. Free-ranging cattle graze on grass, which contains a lot of cellulose. Cattle cannot digest cellulose, so there are micro-organisms in their rumen (stomach) that can digest cellulose. The fermentation that takes place in their rumen releases methane. However, scientists have discovered that the amount of methane that cattle belch is affected by their diet. Cattle fed with grain produce five times less methane per kilogram of meat compared with cattle grazing on grass. Feeding cattle grain suits intensive barn-based systems, but the trend today is towards more extensive grazing on grassland. However, cattle could be fed supplements, which inhibit the methane-producing bacteria in the rumen.

## CFCs

In 1985, the 'ozone hole' was discovered over Antarctica and in 1986 NASA scientists proved that CFCs were responsible for destroying ozone at high altitudes. As a result, there was an international agreement, called the Montreal Protocol, for the production of CFCs to be phased out. Today, CFCs have been replaced by chemicals that do not damage the ozone. However, there is a black market (illegal trade) in CFCs, which are still being used in some countries that have not signed the Montreal Protocol. The problem with CFCs is that they are very long-lived molecules and they remain in the atmosphere for many decades. The effect of CFCs produced over the last 30 years is still being felt, for both ozone depletion and the greenhouse effect.

The rice plants are planted by hand into waterlogged soil. The water level is kept high by the use of banks around the paddy field. Later in the growing season the soils are allowed to dry out. It is during the wet phase that most of the methane production takes place.

# Global warming – fact or fiction?

There is a minority of scientists and politicians who support the case that **global warming** is unlikely, or that if there is global warming it will not happen as quickly as predicted by others. Their arguments include:

- The length of global climate records is too short to be meaningful. Most records only date back 100 years or so and many are unreliable. An increase of 0.5 degrees Celsius could be a result of natural variation. Recent increases in temperature could be due to world-wide urbanization and its 'heat-effect'. Measurements taken in urban areas reflect the increased use of energy and local pollution. Recent research using data from rural weather stations and satellites in the USA actually shows a slight decrease between 1920 and 1990.

- Global temperatures have been slow to respond to 250 years of increasing greenhouse gases. Some scientists argue that the current levels of carbon dioxide in the atmosphere should have increased global temperatures by 2 degrees Celsius already. During the 1930s there was a short period of global warming, which caused widespread droughts, for example the Dust Bowl in the southern USA. This period of global warming occurred before the massive increase in the use of fossil fuels after the Second World War.

- Any warming could be offset by increasing water vapour levels and cloud formation. A warmer atmosphere could hold more water vapour. This would condense to form clouds. An increase in cloud cover could reflect back incoming **radiation** and lead to lower daytime temperatures. However, at night the reverse is true and more heat is trapped.

- Incoming solar radiation is variable. The Sun goes through cycles of solar activity. Areas of high activity are called sunspots and these occur on approximately 11 and 100 year cycles. The 'Little Ice Age' (1430–1850) is believed to have occurred during a period of minimal sunspot activity, while the warm years of the 1930s occurred during a sunspot. The cycle is currently at a maximum.

- Oceans have a role to play in controlling global warming. Oceans disperse heat and store heat. The heat capacity of the oceans is probably 1000 times greater than that of the atmosphere. The deepest parts of the ocean are very slow to respond to increases in temperature. Recent observations of ocean water at 2500 metres indicates that it has not increased in temperature.

# A waste of money?

There are some scientists who do not believe that global warmimg will have the impact that has been predicted. The greenhouse 'sceptics' believe that spending vast sums of money on combating the increases in greenhouse gases will be a waste. It will reduce economic growth and necessitate a major change in lifestyle. They think that government policies have been influenced by environmentalists who predict a frightening future unless global warming is reversed.

The sceptics believe in 'wait and see'. They want clear evidence of global warming before the changes are made. In response, people who believe that global warming is a fact warn that action needs to be taken now and it will be too late to wait ten years until there is proof.

During the Dust Bowl period in the 1930s, droughts and unusually high temperatures destroyed what had been productive farmlands in south-central USA.

# Living with global warming

It is likely that within a few decades people will be living in a world that is warmer than today and this will affect their lifestyle. Buildings will need to become increasingly energy efficient and, where possible, will make use of alternative energy sources such as wind and solar energy. Agriculture and industry will have to change, too. Predictions suggest that **fossil fuels** will still be abundant and relatively cheap up until 2020. But after this time, the supplies of oil and gas could start to fall and prices will increase. Inevitably there will have to be changes. Cars will not be powered by oil. Instead people will be driving cars powered by hydrogen or **fuel cells** (an energy store rather like a battery).

## Conserving the water supply

**Climate** change is expected to affect both evaporation and rainfall. In those areas where evaporation increases more than rainfall, the soil will become drier, lake levels will drop, and rivers will carry less water. This could affect shipping, **hydroelectric** power generation and water quality. There could be reduced water supplies for agricultural, residential, and industrial uses. In California's Central Valley, for example, melting snow provides much of the summer water supply. The snow melts over a number of months, providing a steady supply of water. Warmer temperatures would cause the snow to melt earlier and quicker.

Rainfall may be concentrated in heavy storms and this would lead to increased flooding without increasing water availability. Worldwide, plans are being drawn up to reduce the vulnerability to floods along major rivers, such as the Rhine. In some areas it will be impossible to stop rivers from flooding. In such cases, it is better to move people off the flood plains, remove the flood defences and allow the river to flood. This may prevent flooding along more populated parts of the river.

New flood alleviation measures on the River Ouse are an attempt to protect the historic English city of York.

# Building design

A house of the future will have to be designed to withstand extreme weather such as violent storms, strong winds and heatwaves. A future house may be built on stilts to protect the house from flooding and allow cooling breezes to pass under and through the house in summer. Large windows on the side facing the Sun will let in sunlight and trap heat. In contrast, the shady side will have just a few windows and these will be small to minimize heat loss. Some of the roofing tiles may be replaced with specially designed tile-like photovoltaic panels, which convert light energy into electric energy. The house could be protected from the wind by windbreaks. These could be produced by planting fast-growing trees, such as willows, or by building a frame on the wind side of the house over which climbing plants could grow. The plants would break the wind and shade the house in summer. However, wind is a useful source of **renewable** energy so there may be a small wind **turbine** in the garden. Rainwater from the roof will be collected in underground tanks to be used in summer, and dirty water from sinks and baths will be recycled to flush the toilets.

## Going it alone

In 1993, Portland in Oregon became the first US city to put in place its own carbon dioxide reduction plan. Its goal was to cut emissions to 20 per cent below the 1988 level by 2010. The programme included synchronizing traffic lights to keep traffic flowing, planting 75,000 acres of trees, buying low carbon dioxide vehicles for the city's fleet of buses and trucks, improving the public transport system and improving recycling. Some measures have been highly successful. There are 30 per cent more people using public transport and car commuters are down 15 per cent. The amount of solid waste produced from homes is down 13 per cent. Unfortunately, the city's carbon dioxide emissions have risen because of an unexpected boom in the number of people moving into the area.

## Living without fossil fuels

Iceland is using its **geothermal** energy source – that is, heat from hot rocks – to meet all of its energy needs. Iceland is a volcanic island and hot water bubbles to the surface in the form of geysers and hot springs. This inexhaustible source of geothermal energy, together with some hydroelectric power, supplies 90 per cent of Iceland's electricity. Iceland is now attempting to become the first country to eliminate the use of fossil fuels completely and get all of its energy from clean, renewable sources. Central to this plan is the hydrogen fuel cell. Fortunately, there is plenty of clean energy to carry out electrolysis to produce the hydrogen. Over the next decade the country's vehicles will be converted to run on hydrogen fuel cells.

## Water harvesting

In India, trapping and storing water is essential for survival. In some parts of India the rains are heavy but infrequent. The **monsoon** rains arrive at a particular time each year and mark the start of the rainy season. This is followed by months of hot, dry weather. In the past, people traditionally set aside huge areas of land to capture the rainwater. Over the last century these systems have fallen into disrepair. Now communities are relearning how to trap the water that falls during the monsoon season and to store it for use in the dry season. By combining traditional and modern methods it will be possible for villages to have drinking water all year round.

Hydrogen refill cannisters will be available from service stations around the country. Later, there will be a programme of replacing conventional chemical batteries with fuel cells to power mobile homes and buildings that are not on the **national grid**. If this programme is successful and Icelanders can free themselves of a dependency on fossil fuels, then there is hope that other countries will be able to achieve similar success.

*'It is the Government's policy to promote increased utilization of renewable energy resources in harmony with the environment. One possible approach towards this goal is production of environmentally friendly fuels for powering vehicles and fishing vessels. Liquid hydrogen is an example of such a fuel.'*

The Icelandic Ministry of Industry and Commerce

The Blue Lagoon in Iceland is a popular tourist spot. The geothermal power station beside the lagoon takes hot water and steam from the ground to generate electricity. The waste hot water is pumped into the bathing lagoon, which is used by tourists and locals alike.

# Conclusion

Climate change is a global problem requiring action from everybody. Countries have to work together to share technologies and resources to lower **greenhouse gas** emissions and reduce the threat of global climate change.

## One person's solution

Norman Myers is a British ecologist and environmental economist. For many years he was interested in the mass extinction of species that was taking place during the 1970s. Today he advises governments on ways to limit the damage being done to the natural environment by human activities. Myers believes that the problems facing the world can be tackled using the following approaches:

- Reduce the rate of human population increase by making contraception available to everybody.
- Reduce wasteful consumption. People living in developing countries use a fraction of the fossil fuel used in developed countries. For example, the population in Bangladesh may be increasing by 2.4 million people each year, which is 20 times more than the UK, but each person in the UK produces 50 times more carbon dioxide.
- Increase the price of **fossil fuels**. The cost of petrol/gasoline at the pump does not reflect its true cost in terms of the damage it does to the environment. For example, if the costs of widespread pollution, road congestion, traffic accidents and global warming were reflected in the pump price, Americans would be paying as much as US$7 to US$8 per gallon. Higher prices would reduce consumption.
- Remove the **subsidies** on fossil fuels. Fossil fuels are heavily subsidized and this makes it difficult for renewable sources of energy to compete. In the USA, for example, for every US$1 of subsidy for wind power or solar energy, there are more than US$10 for fossil fuels.
- Reduce poverty in the developing world. Many people are so poor that they are forced to clear their forests for fuel wood and crops. This leads to the extinction of many species of plants and animals. By helping these people to get out of poverty, valuable habitats, such as the rainforest, could be saved.

In the short term there is not much chance of halting **global warming**, even if the targets of the Kyoto **Protocol** are met (see page 10). The treaty requires only small reductions in carbon dioxide emissions to have taken place by 2012. By that time a great deal of damage will have already been done. However, it is possible to slow things down. In addition, governments will have to solve the problem of providing electricity to developing countries without sending greenhouse gas emissions sky high. This will be possible if emissions from coal-burning power stations are cut drastically and by moving to **renewable** energy sources.

Action today could keep the global climate from eventually reaching an unstable tipping point and it may begin to reverse the warming trend within the next 100 years. Experts have shown people that global warming is really happening. Governments, businesses and people are having to learn to use this information in ways that could eventually put the brakes on global warming.

The most likely scenario is that the world will get warmer. People will have to learn how to survive in a warmer world. They will have to cope with more extreme weather events, flooding and drought. There may be food and water shortages. People living in developed countries may have to accept that their lifestyle and standard of living will need to change.

*'We live at an unprecedented time, and we live as a privileged people. No other human generation could ever encounter such a supreme challenge as ours. We have it in our hands to save millions of species that without our help will disappear into oblivion.'*

Norman Myers, British ecologist
and environmental economist

# Timeline

**1810– 1830** Britain experiences some of its coldest winters. Frost Fairs are held on the River Thames when it freezes over.

**1930s** Some of the southern US states experience a decade of droughts and crop failures. Sandstorms are common and a huge area of land is nicknamed the Dust Bowl.

**1988** World Meteorological Organization and United Nations Environment Programme establish The Intergovernmental Panel on Climate Change (**IPCC**).

**1990** The IPCC's first report is published. It recommends the launch of negotiations on a global climate change agreement. The Second World Climate Conference also calls for the launch of negotiations. The UN General Assembly opens negotiations on a Framework Convention on Climate Change and establishes an Intergovernmental Negotiating Committee to conduct these.

**1991** Mount Pinatubo erupts, pumping vast quantities of ash and dust into the atmosphere.

**1992** Average global temperature falls slightly as a result of the dust in the atmosphere.

The UN Framework Convention on Climate Change is adopted in New York.

The Earth Summit takes place in Rio de Janeiro, Brazil. The UN Framework Convention on Climate Change is opened for signature.

**1994** The UN Framework Convention on Climate Change enters into force, after receiving 50 signatures.

**1995** The IPCC publishes its Second Assessment Report on the science of climate change. Its findings emphasize the need for strong policy action.

**1997**  Climate talks take place in Kyoto, Japan. The Kyoto **Protocol** is drawn up. It requires Annex 1 countries (industrialized countries) to reduce their carbon dioxide emissions to the level that existed in 1990 by the year 2012.

**1998**  The Kyoto Protocol is opened for signature at UN headquarters in New York. Over a one-year period, it receives 84 signatures.

1998 proves to be the hottest year on record.

**2000**  Many countries suffer from freak weather events, including flooding in the UK, Northern Europe, Mozambique and India, and record-breaking summer temperatures in parts of the Mediterranean.

Major companies including BP, Alcan and DuPont join with Environmental Defense to launch the Partnership for Climate Action. They pledge to reduce their **greenhouse gas** emissions to levels meeting or below those set by the Kyoto Protocol.

**2001**  The IPCC publishes its third report, which clearly states that the trend towards a warmer climate has begun.

180 governments agree to implement the Kyoto Protocol. The USA decides not to sign, claiming that the Protocol would harm US industry.

**2002**  Earth Summit 2002 takes place, ten years after the first Earth Summit in 1992.

**2005**  Annex 1 Parties must have made demonstrable progress in achieving their commitments under the Kyoto Protocol. Talks for the next round of commitments (post-2012) are launched

# Glossary

**atmosphere** layer of air that surrounds the Earth

**biodiversity** range of different plant and animal species

**biomass** mass of living organisms

**bleaching** loss of algae from corals that causes the corals to turn white

**boreal** describing forests that grow in northern regions of the world such as Canada and Siberia

**carbon sink** part of the carbon cycle where large quantities of carbon are built up, for example, in the wood of trees, in calcium carbonate rocks and in animal species

**catalytic converter** device fitted onto a car's exhaust to reduce air pollutants, such as carbon monoxide and nitrogen oxide

**CFC** chlorofluorocarbon, a gas used in refrigerators and aerosols. Production has now ceased in most parts of the world.

**climate** usual pattern of weather that is averaged over a long period of time

**condense** to change from gas to liquid, for example water vapour changing to liquid water

**deforestation** felling of large areas of forests

**ecosystem** community of interacting organisms and their physical environment

**El Niño** periodic weather event in which the waters of the Eastern Pacific Ocean off the coast of South America become much warmer than normal and disturb weather patterns across the region

**exhaust** waste gases pumped out by engines and chimneys of power stations and industrial plants, etc.

**fossil fuel** coal, oil or natural gas, which are formed from plant and animal remains trapped in rocks

**fuel cell** device that converts energy. Electricity and heat are produced when the fuels within the fuel cell react together.

**geothermal** describing energy from the earth's hot core

**glacier** mass of ice formed by the build-up of snow over hundreds of years

**global warming** increase in the temperature of the Earth, caused by the build-up of greenhouse gases in the atmosphere

**greenhouse effect** natural trapping of heat energy by gases, such as carbon dioxide and methane, which are present in the atmosphere

**greenhouse gas** gas which traps heat in the atmosphere and keeps the earth warm

**Gulf Stream** warm current that flows from the Gulf of Mexico across the Atlantic to northern Europe

**hydroelectric** describing electricity produced using falling water

**Industrial Revolution** period during which industry develops rapidly as a result of advances in technology. This took place in Britain during the late 18th and early 19th centuries.

**IPCC** Intergovernmental Panel on Climate Change

**malaria** dangerous parasitic disease caused by a microscopic single-celled organism carried by the female *Anopheles* mosquito

**monsoon** heavy rains which occur at the same time each year

**national grid** network of power lines that links up all the power stations in a country and which distributes electricity over a large area

**ozone** molecule that consists of three oxygen atoms. Most ozone is found in the stratosphere, where it absorbs ultraviolet light. Ozone is damaged by CFCs.

**parasite** organism that lives on or in another organism, doing that organism some harm, for example tape worms that live in dogs

**permafrost** permanent frozen ground in the Arctic

**photosynthesis** process by which plants make food using light energy, carbon dioxide and water

**protocol** terms of a treaty which have been agreed and signed by all parties

**radiation** emitting of energy as particles or waves. Heat and light are two forms of radiant energy.

**radiosonde** balloon for measuring weather high in the atmosphere

**renewable** describing something that can be replaced or regrown, for example trees, or a source of energy that never runs out, such as the sun or wind

**resources** raw materials that are used to make things, for example wood, oil and gold

**respiration** process by which food is broken down in cells using oxygen and producing carbon dioxide

**ruminant** type of herbivorous animal that has a specially adapted stomach that can digest the cellulose in plants

**satellite** any small object that orbits a larger one. Artificial satellites carry instruments for scientific study and communication. Moons are natural satellites.

**simulation** computer model of a process based on real facts

**subsidy** money used by a government to keep the price of something artificially low

**temperate** describing regions of the world that have mild climates and seasons

**thermal** relating to heat

**tropical** hot and often wet regions of the world near the Equator

**tundra** vast, treeless plain in the Arctic with a marshy surface lying over the permafrost

**turbine** motor or engine, driven by a flow of steam, water, wind or gas, which generates electricity

**ultraviolet radiation** invisible part of the light spectrum

# Sources of information

## Further reading

*Global Warming*, Frances Drake, OUP, 2000
*Global Warming: The Complete Briefing*, John Houghton, CUP, 1997
*Global Warming: The Greenpeace Report*, OUP, 1990
Magazines such as *Biological Sciences Review* and *New Scientist* also publish articles on topics related to global warming.

## Websites

**www.ipcc.ch** The website of the Intergovernmental Panel on Climate Change (IPCC), where you can download the reports of the scientists. The reports are very technical and are not easy to read, but they give lots of information.

**www.wmo.ch** The website of the World Meteorological Organization (WMO), where you can find out how meteorological data is collected and learn about some of the international programmes.

**www.epa.gov/globalwarming/** The US Environmental Protection Agency's site on global warming with lots of factual information and links to other sites.

**www.globalwarming.org** An informative US-based site on global warming, with articles, data and links.

**www.unep.ch/conventions/info/infoindex.htm** The United Nations Framework on Climate Change can be accessed from here. This website provides information on the climate change negotiations.

**www.dar.csiro.au** The website of the Australian Climate Research Centre provides answers to some of the questions on global warming and climate change.

**www.pewclimate.org** The website of the Pew Centre, an organization in the US that covers issues of climate change and how people can respond to the changes.

# Index

atmosphere 6, 12, 14, 20, 38, 50

biodiversity, loss of 32–3
biological changes 9, 32–7
biomass 47
building design 52

carbon cycle 17
carbon dioxide/carbon dioxide emissions 5, 7, 10, 11, 14, 15, 16–17, 22, 23, 30, 38, 39, 42, 43, 46, 47, 48, 50, 54, 56, 57
carbon sinks 17, 46
carbon tax 43
cars 11, 43–5, 52
catalytic converters 43
CFCs (chlorofluorocarbons) 14, 15, 19, 48, 49
climate change 5, 6, 9, 21, 23, 24–31, 38, 53, 56
Climate Technology Initiative (CTI) 45
cloud cover 23, 50
coastal erosion 27, 30
coral bleaching 30, 34–5
coral islands 22, 27, 30

deforestation 16, 17, 38, 46, 57
desertification 27, 33
developing countries 11, 38, 45, 56, 57
droughts 9, 25, 27, 29, 35, 37, 50
dust 27

El Niño and La Niña 28–9, 35
electricity generation 39, 40, 41, 42, 43, 45, 53, 54, 55, 56
energy efficiency 38, 40–1, 52
extinction 32–3, 34

feedback mechanisms 23
flooding 4, 31, 36, 53
food production 35, 36, 49
forests 16, 17, 26, 33, 46–7
fossil fuels 7, 16, 18, 38, 39, 43, 46, 50, 52, 54, 57
fuel cells 44, 45, 52, 54, 55

geothermal energy 54, 55
glaciers 9, 27, 31
global average temperatures 5, 6, 7, 14, 24, 25, 50
global warming 5, 6, 8, 14, 19, 20
  arguments against 11, 50–1
  biological changes 9, 32–7
  climatic consequences 9, 24–31
  combating 38–49, 56, 57
  living with 52–5
greenhouse effect 5, 12, 13, 14, 49
greenhouse gases 5, 6, 7, 9–10, 13, 14–19, 23, 25, 31, 38, 39, 43, 44, 45, 51, 56
Gulf Stream 28

health 19, 36, 37
heatwaves 4, 35, 37
hurricanes 21, 27
hydrogen gas 45, 52, 54, 55

ice sheets 6, 8, 22, 27, 31
Intergovernmental Panel on Climate Change (IPCC) 8, 9, 24

Kyoto Protocol 9–10, 38, 41, 45, 56

'Little Ice Age' 6, 50

methane 5, 14, 18, 48–9
mosquitoes 36
mountains 34

nitrous oxide 14, 18
nuclear power 43

ocean currents 28–9
oceans 17, 27–9, 50
ozone layer depletion 19, 21, 49

permafrost 9, 26
pests and diseases 36–7
photosynthesis 14, 17, 35, 46

radiation 12, 13, 23, 27, 50
rainfall 4, 9, 26, 29, 53, 54
renewable energy 38, 41–3, 52, 56

satellite monitoring 20–1, 50
sea levels 9, 24, 27, 30–1
seas, fertilizing 47
semi-arid areas 32, 33
solar energy 40, 41, 42, 44, 52

tundra 26, 33

vegetation cover 16–17, 26–7, 33, 34, 46–7

water supply 53, 54
water vapour 14, 23, 26, 50
weather data 6, 20–3, 50
weather predictions 21, 22–3
weather stations 20, 50
wind power 41–2, 52
World Meteorological Organization (WM) 20, 21